F
Changes

by Adrian Powers

HOUGHTON MIFFLIN BOSTON

PHOTOGRAPHY CREDITS: Cover (t) © Design Pics Inc./Alamy, (b) © Jon Riley; 1 © Jupiter Images/BananaStock/Alamy; 2 © Jon Riley; 3 © Stephen Simpson/Getty Images; 4 (l) © Blickwinkel/Alamy, (m) © PureStock/Jupiter Images, (r) © Visual&Written SL/Alamy; 5 © PhotoDisc; 6 © ROB & SAS/Corbis; 7 © Jupiter Images/BananaStock/Alamy; 8 © Stockbyte/Getty Images; 9 © Comstock Images, (inset) © Stockbyte; 10 © Digital Vision/Getty Images

Printed in China

ISBN-13: 978-0-547-02828-6
ISBN-10: 0-547-02828-8

12 13 14 15 0940 17 16 15 14
4500496268

Fall is the season that comes before winter. It is a season that brings many changes.

We see fall when we look at trees. We feel fall when the air is cool. We can hear fall when dry leaves crunch under our feet.

In the fall, it gets dark early. The days feel shorter because there is less sunlight each day.

The weather changes in the fall, too. In some places, the air gets cool. In other places, it rains a lot.

In the fall, animals get ready for winter. They put away food to eat during the winter. They look for warm, dry places to sleep when the weather changes. Some animals sleep for the whole winter!

In the fall, the leaves on many trees change colors. First, they change from green to yellow.

Then they turn red and orange.

Next, the leaves turn brown and drop to the ground.

At the start of fall, the air still feels warm. Only a few leaves drop to the ground.

A few weeks later, the air is cool. Many leaves fall from the trees.

When there are a lot of leaves on the ground, people rake them into piles. Sometimes kids like to jump in the piles!

By the end of fall, many tree branches are empty. They will grow new green leaves in the spring. But not all trees lose their leaves in the fall.

Some trees are different. They have needles instead of leaves. The needles stay green all year. They do not change colors or drop to the ground in the fall.

At the end of the season, we can see and feel that fall is almost over. The air feels colder. The days seem shorter. Many animals are asleep. Winter will be here soon.

Responding

TARGET SKILL **Cause and Effect**

What happens in the fall? Why does it happen? Make a chart.

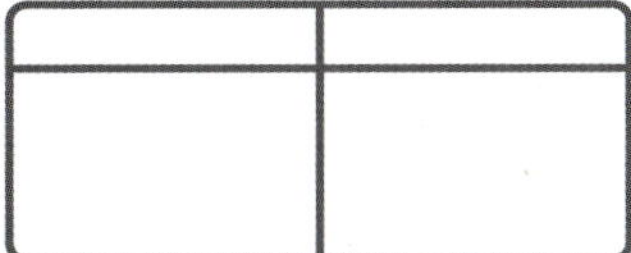

Talk About It

Text to Self What is your favorite season? Why is it your favorite?

WORDS TO KNOW

down	**grow**
fall	**new**
goes	**open**
green	**yellow**

TARGET SKILL Cause and Effect

Tell what happens and why.

TARGET STRATEGY Visualize

Picture what is happening as you read.

GENRE **Informational text** gives facts about a topic.